The Book

of

Contemplation

The Book
of
Contemplation

77 Words
*for Thought
and Meditation*

H. Wyatt Rollins

Cover design by Amy C. King
Cover photograph by Corbis
Text design by Amy C. King

Library of Congress Cataloging-in-Publication Data
Rollins, H. Wyatt (Henderson Wyatt), 1972-
   The book of contemplation : 77 words for thought and
   meditation / H. Wyatt Rollins.
   p. cm.
   ISBN 0-9742405-4-0
   1. Spiritual life. 2. Contemplation. I. Title.

   BL624.R63 2005
   158.1'28--dc22   2005002352

Published by
BlueBridge
An imprint of United Tribes Media Inc.
240 West 35th Street, Suite 500
New York, NY 10001
www.bluebridgebooks.com

Printed in the United States of America
10 9 8 7 6 5 4 3 2 1

Preface

The Book of Contemplation is unlike other books. It will not tell you what to do or think or believe, or what message you should take away from it. Instead, it is a simple and gentle invitation: it invites you to contemplate seventy-seven words. These words are among the most important, most essential, most transcendent words in life, and each one has been chosen very carefully for inclusion here. It is an invitation to open yourself up to the ideas and principles embodied in each word, and to embrace their many inherent possibilities and challenges. This book is really about *you*, your experiences, your wisdom, your spirituality. *You* are the one who brings this book to life, who fills each word with the unique beauty, meaning, and power that lie within you.

So open this book at any time and to any page. You may choose to read and contemplate only one word at a time, or two or three, or all of the seventy-seven words in one sitting. Just follow your intuition—wherever you are, and whenever you feel like it. You may share and discuss these words with others. You may disagree with some of the words included. You may add words that are meaningful to you. However you decide to use *The Book of Contemplation*, my sincere wish is that it will continuously bring into focus and inspire your attitudes, beliefs, and choices in life, and therefore be of lasting joy and value to you.

H. Wyatt Rollins

Light

Stillness

Humility

Kindness

Knowledge

Patience

Universe

Commitment

Awareness

Body

Family

Integrity

Gratitude

Nature

Simplicity

Trust

Eternity

Work

Freedom

Creation

Heart

Service

Power

Earth

Gift

Courage

Forgiveness

Age

Spirit

Success

Home

Change

Being

Community

Value

Passion

Respect

Beauty

Love

Balance

Compassion

Friendship

Time

Journey

Discipline

Play

Heaven

Justice

Mercy

Mind

God

Perseverance

Happiness

Blessing

Peace

Grace

Tolerance

Action

Space

Honesty

Soul

Harmony

Choice

Truth

Worship

Silence

Faith

Health

Loyalty

Attitude

Responsibility

Wisdom

Now

Joy

Understanding

Life

Hope

The 77 Words

Light	Forgiveness	Happiness
Stillness	Age	Blessing
Humility	Spirit	Peace
Kindness	Success	Grace
Knowledge	Home	Tolerance
Patience	Change	Action
Universe	Being	Space
Commitment	Community	Honesty
Awareness	Value	Soul
Body	Passion	Harmony
Family	Respect	Choice
Integrity	Beauty	Truth
Gratitude	Love	Worship
Nature	Balance	Silence
Simplicity	Compassion	Faith
Trust	Friendship	Health
Eternity	Time	Loyalty
Work	Journey	Attitude
Freedom	Discipline	Responsibility
Creation	Play	Wisdom
Heart	Heaven	Now
Service	Justice	Joy
Power	Mercy	Understanding
Earth	Mind	Life
Gift	God	Hope
Courage	Perseverance	

Epilogue

The idea for this book was years in the making, and is the result of a chain of both happy and painful personal experiences. Sometimes it still amazes me that it has now become a real book, and that anyone can use it anytime and anywhere they wish. But here it is, in your hands, and I want to share with you how it came to be.

As a child I was introduced to golf and taught to play it. By the time I was a teenager I was competing all over the United States in junior tournaments, and after high school I landed a spot in a highly ranked collegiate golf program. In my second year of college I made the traveling squad, and we finished the year as one of the top five teams in the nation. I was showing great promise, and a career in professional golf was becoming a real possibility.

But something was wrong. I was on my way, but I wasn't sure where I was going, or why. I was beginning to wonder if I really wanted to get there. The more I questioned my life, the more its drive and purpose faded. And worse, I couldn't stop it. It was occurring beyond my control, almost with a will of its own. Soon I didn't want to play golf anymore, nor do anything else. By the time I turned twenty, I found myself in a deep life crisis.

Most of the people in my life thought I was losing my mind, although some recognized that I was in tremendous pain. But no one, not even I, knew or understood what really was happening to me. A bleak emptiness had first enveloped and then consumed me, making me question deep inside if I wanted to carry on living any longer. I needed a fundamental change. *I* needed to change.

But my life was spiritually empty at the time. I had been raised in a mainstream church, but the faith I had encountered there hadn't made an impression on me. I was spiritually ignorant and inexperienced, and I didn't know where to begin. As my condition worsened and I groped in the dark for some kind of direction, the most horrible sensation came over me, the stubborn remnants of which would last for years. I felt like I was falling, endlessly, hopelessly, into nothingness. I was spiraling totally out of control.

Almost unconsciously I began to realize that I had to find out, for myself, the purpose of life. If there was a purpose, I told myself, if God did exist, nothing else mattered. If nothing was there, nothing mattered anyway. That question was at the core of my pain, and I couldn't focus on anything else. So I began a nearly decadelong search for God and meaning among the world's countless spiritual and philosophical writings. I read and thought and wrote endlessly, following my instincts, looking for the truth, looking for God. My outer life was on hold, as if I had disappeared, and I had no idea how my inner search would end or if it ever could. In truth, it didn't matter to me one way or another.

Around that time, a good friend of mine had taken a trip to Italy. While he was browsing through the sidewalk shops of some quaint village in the countryside, he came across a beautiful handmade, leather-bound journal. The paper was rough and natural, the leather cover was attached with string, and the overall effect was simple elegance. He bought it and gave it to me as a gift after his return.

I had never seen anything quite like this little journal before. It had a sort of exotic, hand-crafted beauty and mystique to it that I loved. It was especially meaningful to me that it was a gift from my friend, with whom I had enjoyed countless conversations on life and meaning. This journal was a treasure to me, and I only wanted to fill its pages with something truly worthwhile. Since I didn't have anything I thought was worthy to write in it, I put the journal on my shelf and didn't touch it for a long time.

Several years later—I was now in my late twenties but still in the throes of my all-consuming search—my longing took on a new quality. I had by now come to believe that life does have a purpose, and that God does exist. But how could I, personally, draw closer to God? I just knew I wanted the *experience* of God, the connection, as often and as intensely as I could get it, because it had become the most beautiful and powerful experience in my life.

I longed for an aid to help me connect to God, and also to assist me in my pursuit of the spiritual principles and teachings I had discovered over the years. What I needed was a way to remind myself of all I had learned and come to believe in, to express its essence and to focus my attention more sharply on it.

One day, I began to distill everything I had read and learned. On loose sheets of paper, I wrote down the thoughts and principles that I felt were of fundamental importance, part of the foundation of my developing spiritual life. Most were verses or ideas derived from the ancient sacred texts of the world. Others were spiritual truths I had arrived at from my own experience and understanding. Still others were principles of such importance, power, and depth that they could best be expressed by just one single word. My goal was to combine all of these notes into a collection I could carry with me, literally and figuratively, as a singular guidebook for my own spiritual journey.

Soon I realized that only the handmade journal my friend had given me years earlier would be worthy to record all these thoughts and concepts. I pulled it off the shelf and began for the first time to write on its empty pages. I transcribed all of my notes into it, taking a full page of the journal for every individual thought, verse, or word. I called it my "Book of Contemplation." When I was finished I felt that I had done something worthwhile for myself, and had finally found a worthwhile purpose for the journal. As I turned its pages, one core principle after another struck my eye and my heart, allowing me to connect with God in a beautiful and powerful new way.

But as the days passed and I read my journal again and again, I began to realize it wasn't quite finished. Yet another, further distillation was possible and desirable to arrive at the true essence of it all. A book with a single word on every page, while almost uncomfortably simple, could become a guide for any seeker, no matter what their spiritual background. My leather-bound journal could be transformed into a work with wide appeal and application. So I began the painstaking selection process for each word. I wanted to capture the core principles of our very being, carefully choosing the one word that best conveys a particular principle. In the end I arrived at these seventy-seven words.

Over the weeks and months of that selection process and the subsequent development of *The Book of Contemplation*, I slowly began to come out of my long period of struggle. The energy and purpose I had gained in creating this humble spiritual statement broke through my isolation and allowed me to reenter the world. Just as I had dropped my outer life as a youth to search for purpose and for God, I now picked it up again to try to live it meaningfully. At the heart of that effort are the words in this book.